WORKBOOK

For

HOW TO DO THE WORK

Recognize your patterns, heal from your past and create your self

DR. NICOLE LePERA

THE HOLISTIC PSYCHOLOGIST

Copyright © 2021 by: Roger Press

Table of Contents

ABOUT THE AUTHOR

Dr. Nicole LePera was trained in The New School for Social Research and studied clinical psychology at the Cornell University.

This universal psychologist resides in Los Angeles and continues to expand her reach even in the online space with her huge Instagram presence and The Self Healers Circle, where she shares her means to total transformation, alongside a constantly growing community of Self-Healers.

INTRODUCTION

A PRIMER ON HOLISTIC PSYCHOLOGY

This piece aims to give you the tools that will enable you better understand and connect the multifaceted interconnectedness of your mind, body, and soul. This will encourage a more authentic, deeper, and significant relationship with yourself, others, and within our society at large.

In life, many individuals have all they want and need. We can say they have the best of lives and can be the envy of many. But deep inside these "so-called" successful or seemingly fulfilled lots are wells of emptiness, detachment, impassivity, physically drained individuals, and a myriad of other challenges when you get closer. So many are up and about in an efficient guise, but all that drama is all in a bid to distract ourselves from intensely ingrained unanswered feelings.

Everyone on planet earth hits rock-bottom, there comes a time when we are faced with pain, suffering, trauma, and eventually our actual Self. It is in that very moment that we either evolve stronger or allow our challenges to bring us to our death. It is in pain that pleasure comes, it is in finding ourselves again that we are truly reborn. As soon as the light finds expression within, it reveals so much that we have tried to bury, and then change comes. The emergence of the change spoken of by the author brought about a psychological, physical, and spiritual awakening that led to a global movement to date.

Dr. Nicole tackled her physical health first by changing her physical routine to be more active and her mindset on mental wellness. She later discovered that when the mind, body, and soul doesn't function as one, it can show up physically as sickness and dysregulation. Also, we can alter the functionality of our genes by our thought patterns and daily activities.

Secondly, she realized the huge spiritual effects that stress and unfavorable experiences that occur in childhood hamper on the body's nervous system till old age. As Dr. Nicole transformed, it affected her choices positively and with time she began to *"reparent"* her inner child and began to relate with the world with the utmost level of emotional maturity.

This book; "How to Do the Work" is a piece of representational evidence that Holistic Psychology works in promoting the wellness of the mind, body, and soul. It is a liberating movement fueled by regular practice of building your wellness by healing from the past that hurts you, breaking negative patterns, and making your conscious Self.

THE BENEFITS OF THIS WORK;

- It concentrates on the body, mind, and soul in a bid to rebalance the body, nervous system and heal unsolved emotional wounds.
- Empowers you to evolve into the person you've always been at your best.
- You begin to perceive your physical and psychological symptoms as messages, instead of long-term diagnoses rid of solutions only left to be managed.
- This work gets to the origin of stress, severe pain, fatigue, gut dysregulation, anxiety, and nervous system imbalances, which we have ignored or disregarded by traditional Western medicine.
- This work provides a candid explanation as to why a majority of us feel disconnected, stuck, or lost.
- This work serves as a practical tool to help you in building new habits, understand the behavior of others more, and eliminate the idea that your worth is only determined by others or things asides from your humble self.
- This work will help you in connecting with your authentic Self.
- This work encircles various aspects of other numerous modalities such as psychology, neuroscience, and then mindfulness and spirituality drills to promote a very operational and sustainable technique for healing and wellness.

Here is a mental book and guide for your general body wellness, if you are still struggling to see an alternate reality than the present one you are in, then you need more work. Begin to dream of a future unlike what your present looks like, this is a sign that you are ready to move forward.

CHAPTER 1: YOU ARE YOUR OWN BEST HEALER

Everyone has come to a point in their lives when they just want to do the right things. Eat clean (less processed food), become an active member in the gym, add moderation to the hours spent on social media, and more. You are so determined to make it work this time, but then after some days of following the books, mental opposition sets in. Harmful things you have succeeded in staying away from all these weeks now suddenly feel like your ticket for survival.

The drive drops, the courage you began this journey with, is nowhere to be found and all your mental pathways are telling you; is to go back to the status quo where you have built a comfort zone. This conviction begins in the mind, then the body intersects with the feeling of weariness and exhaustion, and then you tell yourself that this is not a possible venture you can sustain. This is very typical of many. A large majority of people feel stuck in their bad habits, destructive behaviors, probable and problematic patterns that have caused them to feel very depressed, lonely, and isolated.

Many have also grown to associate their inability to stick to change with a feeling of worthlessness. It is one thing to be self-aware and single out the behaviors within that are problematic and map out a pathway to change. But this attribute is only present in a few, while much more people dwell in shame and self-hate, for always going back to the habits that are detrimental to them and not having enough will to stay in the change they desire to see.

Many cannot see what the future holds, they are sure of the outcome of the past and always find their way back there, even after the most transformational experiences they may have been exposed to in life. Not being able to stay in change drives many to a crisis that can span out for very long.

Over time, Dr. Nicole discovered that singular transformative experiences and therapy can only help us heal; but change only truly comes when we make new choices daily – now that's the "**work**." What you practice daily, you become a master at it. To achieve total wellness, we must actively engage in the things that promote change on a regular, only then can it be sustainable.

Many others who find it hard to stay in change even after discovering the aspect of their lives that calls for change, seem to find solace in substances, being obsessively angry at little or nothing, or being annoyingly petty serving as a form of distraction from their woes. Addiction doesn't only fall within the bracket of alcohol, sex, gambling, or even drugs... cycles of human emotion are highly addictive too.

Emotional addiction is mostly controlling as we constantly seek or circumvent certain emotional states as a means to deal with trauma.

MIND-BODY-SOUL CONNECTION

There lays a complex link between the human body, their minds, and the functionalities of the nervous system as it concerns mental wellness.

The usual practice of separating the treatment of the mind and body as different entities are what puts a large constrain on Western medicine today. This separation in treatment is what often leaves us more ill or even disrupts the healing process altogether. On the other hand, the indigenous culture has found the link connecting the mind, body, and soul. With help from clairvoyance, they have been able to connect with their inner Self thereby operating with an inner knowing, that the human form comprises interconnected parts.

Conventional Western medicine sees this connection as unscientific, even a French philosopher named René Descartes birthed the concept of "mind-body dualism" in the seventeenth century that lived on for another four hundred years. We tend to treat those who are psychologically sick for only what pertains to that record and nothing more and the same goes for the physically ill.

As we approached the nineteenth century, medicine turned into a field of intervention where physicians didn't bother listening to the human body. For instance, the sign of a health challenge will often lead to surgery or the patient if pumped with preventive drugs with known or unknown side effects. In the advents of reducing the visible symptoms with drugs, we end up causing more harm to the body. This is the "Band-Aid model" which focuses on treating individual symptoms as they come and not at the root causes.

Today the American Psychiatric Association has come up with the *Diagnostic and Statistical Manual of Mental Disorders* (DSM-5), this manual catalog symptom as a means to a disorder, which is often genetic (genetic determinism) or "organic" in origin, not environmental or learned. So this way, people go around believing their sickness is hereditary, it is who they are and they make no attempt at eliminating it, the most they can do is to manage it till death.

THE POWER TO TRANSFORM

Genetic determinism disregards the role of environmental factors, traumas, family backgrounds, or even habits in causing sickness. What we experience in our mind, body, and soul is far beyond our DNA. We need to begin to take ownership of our lives and stop the narrative that our faulty genes are our destiny and there is nothing we can do to change that.

Our inherited genes are not fixed; our very immediate environment can influence the outcome of our genes. The question is — are we ready to do the work? Change is a reality; it can happen if you stick to making it so. We are in charge of our everyday choices; the food we eat, our relationship, and how we live life in general.

Epigenetics (the new biology) condemns genetic determinism and supports that the outcome of our genes is greatly influenced by our environment. It is no longer news that our daily environment largely affects our general health, especially our brain in many ways than we can count. Scholars that have propagated this gospel are biologist Bruce Lipton and Dr. Gabor Maté who talked about how stress leaves a lasting emotional imprint on the brain that leads to many psychological and physical sicknesses.

You can shape your DNA with your daily choices. Whatever your genes are saying isn't the end of the line, they can be altered by the choices we make today.

THE PLACEBO EFFECT
The study of epigenetics opened up a fresh craving for healing, transformation, belief, and the placebo effect which is a terminology that represents something that has the power of an inert substance (like a sugar pill) to enhance the symptoms of illness. Many have overcome the worst of illnesses without medical help and with just a lifestyle change in the right direction. We play down on the strength

of the mind in bringing about general wellness and the placebo effect is a significant testimony that this mainstream science is built on fact.

The placebo effect has helped with conditions like irritable bowel syndrome, even Parkinson's disease, and depression where they were taking sugar pills and thought they were taking antidepressants, and there are records of significant changes recorded. The placebo effect is not only for the sick; it can be infused in enhancing our daily activities just to become better at it. This is the brain pushing the body to do better and sends signals all over the body, hormones, neurochemicals and immune cells are all dispersed, to begin the healing process.

The placebo effect proves that when we decide we are going to be better, most times, we always do. The opposite of the placebo effect is the "nocebo effect". This occurs when our thoughts leave us worse than we formerly were.

HOLISTIC PSYCHOLOGY

Getting the revelation that connects mental and physical health is evolutionary and has contributed to the massive change we experience in medicine today. This interconnectedness of the body, soul, and mind gives room for holistic healing.

The basic tenets of Holistic Psychology are;

1. Healing is a daily event that begins with you. Your healing process needs to start inwards so that it has a solid foundation. We need to be daily committed to this work to see results. Little and consistent steps bring long-term transformation.
2. Not everything is beyond our control, have been empowered by our choices that stimulate healing. With holistic Psychology, we can tap into the power of choice.
3. Change is scary and it threatens our very existence, but holistic tools are very practical and approachable. Regular choices in bits strengthen our venture for change.
4. Having control over your mental wellness empowers you.

- **Lessons**

1. For change to be permanent, start practicing and begin to see the future you desire which is different from your past and present realism.
2. Set small but actionable steps to be carried out daily towards your future goal.

- **Issues surrounding the subject matter**

1. What are your thought patterns, behavior, or emotions that make you repeat those unhealthy patterns? Write them all down, no matter how many they are as identifying them will help to evade them.

_____

_____

_____

_____

_____

_____

_____

_____

_____

_____

_____

_____

_____

_____

2. Do you often break the promises you make to yourself to make new choices and build new habits but often go back to your old ways? Why do you think this often happens to you, what factors are responsible?

_____

_____

_____

_____

_____

_____

_____

_____

_____

3. How often are you often disconnected and distracted from your being and others and also unaware of your immediate environment?

_____

_____

_____

_____

_____

_____

_____

_____

_____

- **Goals**

1. In what aspect of your life would you intend to be intentional about change and why?

_____

_____

_____

_____

_____

_____

_____

_____

_____

_____

_____

2. How do you cope with stress and your feelings, are you overwhelmed by it or otherwise; explain.

_____

_____

_____

_____

_____

_____

_____

_____

_____

_____

_____

_____

- **Action steps**
1. Practice little daily promises to yourself and make sure you keep them.
2. Practice "Future Self Journaling" (FSJ) to help you in documenting your daily practice in other to be free from your subconscious autopilot.
- **Checklist**
1. The old model no longer works, what works is the new model of mental wellness.

2. Intentionally search out the ways you feel stuck and
   seek a way out.

CHAPTER 2: THE CONSCIOUS SELF: BECOMING AWARE

We all must have experienced the feeling of "stuckness" one time or the other in life, as you read this; you might even be stuck to your terrible habits and may have looked for ways to break through them, but nothing seems to be working. The feeling of "stuckness" manifests in attributes like chronic anxiety, severe extremist, highly emotionally reactive, an excessive longing to please others, and even an insatiable desire to be perfect.

The mistake many of us make when we find ourselves in this place is all in a bid to suppress our anxiety and realization that we don't know who we are. So we venture into more harmful activities like doing drugs just to remain sane. But the realization is more dissatisfaction. Individuals who find it impossible to move forward in life are caught up in their reactivity.

The painful truth is that not many people have an actual connection with who we are, but we want others to see us in the light of what we don't even see in ourselves. Where have you ever seen someone give what they do not have? If you crave to be treated in a kind of way and you don't begin to display those attributes first, how then do you want others to know you are to be treated as such?

YOU ARE NOT YOUR THOUGHTS

The fact that you process certain thoughts in your head doesn't automatically mean that you represent the contents of your thought. We have to learn to separate ourselves from our thought patterns; they are not who we are and we cannot stop our minds from roaming.

The fundamental step to healing is to be able to witness our internal world and that is to be Self-aware. This is the first condition to achieve long-term change. Then we can talk about the reparenting process which has to do with meeting your inner child, eliminating the ego, and tackling past and present trauma.

Awakening your conscious awareness is to be fully aware of your present Self. Medically, it is a state of being awake in other to be aware of ourselves and the happenings around us, but to also be empowered enough to make choice decisions for growth. All humans practice thoughts, this may sound absurd to hear, but that is what happens all through the day, in our dreams and our subconscious. From the moment we wake up, till when we go to bed; it's practiced thoughts we all display. We have become so unaware that we practice our thought, this is because we have consistently done this very long and that singular practice is now beyond our awareness.

You are the thinker of your thoughts, but you are not your thoughts. Thoughts are electrochemical reactions that occur due to the unleashing of neurons in the brain. Our thoughts help us to recreate, solve challenges, and create connections. It is in the place of self-awareness that a lot of deep things about Self are revealed and only then can you become the best version of yourself. When you are not in a state of self-awareness, many things go wrong. We become so used to the routine that anything wanting to break the routine cycle is seen as a distraction, discomfort, and worthy of elimination.

Our body and mind are so used to being on autopilot that introducing anything new is perceived as an intruder. No wonder the brain is said to only operate 5 percent of the day in a conscious state.

HOMEOSTATIC IMPULSE

Change is compulsory for all living beings, but it is not a state that we are evolutionarily assembled for. Dwelling in the autopilot phase and resisting any form of change from our body and mind puts us in a homeostatic impulse state. This state is responsible for regulating our physiological functioning ranging from breathing − body temperature − heartbeat which is all automated.

The homeostatic impulse aims to generate balance in the body and body. In the presence of dysregulation, the imbalances can pose a big problem. What the brain truly loves is to cruise on autopilot and stay in its comfort zone all century-long, but a life without growth and advancement is as good as worthless. Routine leaves us stuck in the habits we crave to stop and this can be problematic.

It is important to cultivate the power of our conscious awareness to destroy those default automatic feedbacks. Some activities that help to bring one to a state of self-awareness are yoga and meditation as it helps you to be more aware of the present and great at restructuring the brain.

- **Lessons**
1. You are the thinker of your thoughts, but you are not your thoughts.
2. Our thoughts help us to recreate, solve challenges, and create connections.
3. It is in the place of self-awareness that a lot of deep things about Self are revealed and only then can you become the best version of yourself.
- **Issues surrounding the subject matter**
1. Why does the feeling of "stuckness" manifests in attributes like chronic anxiety, severe extremist, highly emotionally reactive, an excessive longing to please others, and even an insatiable desire to be perfect?

_____

_____

_____

_____

_____

_____

_____

_____

_____

_____

_____

_____

_____

- **Goals**

1. In what ways do you intend to build your consciousness going forward?

_____

_____

_____

_____

_____

_____

_____

_____

_____

2. How do we cultivate the power of our conscious awareness to destroy those default automatic feedbacks from gaining ground in our lives?

_____

_____

_____

_____

_____

_____

_____

_____

_____

_____

_____

_____

_____

- **Action steps**
1. Take out some minutes in your day to practice being focused and present in whatever you're doing.
2. Be in the moment intentionally without your mind forcing you to concentrate on the moment.
3. After practicing, acknowledge what you have given yourself and thank yourself for the time taken to get the work done.
4. Repeat this exercise at least once a day. When you get more comfortable, you'll begin to notice more moments when you can repeat the practice.
- **Checklist**
1. We all practice thoughts.

CHAPTER 3: A NEW THEORY OF TRAUMA

Many experiences a state of dissociation; where they are physically present in their environment but are mentally absent. It is a coping mechanism of mental and physical withdrawal from your immediate environment reacting to constant stress.

The term – "dissociation" was coined by Psychiatrist Pierre Janet, describing it as a "splitting off" of Self. Dissociation is quite common with individuals living with childhood trauma as their best reaction to stress. The violated, exploited, and manhandled try to disconnect from their intuition to be able to live with themselves.

TRAUMA: A MISUNDERSTOOD CONCEPT

Trauma is the product of an extremely tragic event, such as neglect and severe abuse. This kind of event alters the individual's life entirely. The Centers for Disease Control and Prevention offers a scale called the Adverse Childhood Experiences (ACEs) test, this scale is often used by mental health professionals to evaluate the level of trauma in their patients' lives. The ACEs questionnaire consists of ten questions on several types of childhood trauma, including verbal, physical, and sexual abuse as well as events of witnessing such abuse.

The ACEs structure is imperative as it states in clear terms how traumas sustained from childhood leave an eternal trace on our minds and bodies, especially when it is an extremely negative experience, that leaves a lasting dent.

Dr. Bessel van der Kolk, a trauma expert and the author of the trailblazing book *The Body Keeps the Score: Brain, Mind, and Body in the Healing of Trauma*, defines dissociation as a state of knowing and not knowing simultaneously. He also mentioned that individuals who detach, simultaneously recall very little and very much.

Traumatized people try hard to persuade their brain that they can survive what they have experienced but when the brain senses any related danger, the entire system ships a quantifiable amount of stress hormone that triggers hostile emotions, violence, and strong physical perceptions. Presently, the functionality of the body system (organ) is easily predicted by medical practitioners, but what hasn't been figured is the complexity of the human mind and what goes on in the brain, and what compels affection.

Three scientific studies have created new disciplines to help us understand the effects of neglect, psychological trauma, and abuse. They are neuroscience, developmental psychopathology, and interpersonal neurobiology. The first discipline concerns how our brain backs up mental progressions, the second term developmental psychopathology concerns itself with the level of impact the hostile experience hampers on the brain and mind development, while the last term; interpersonal neurobiology studies the level at which our behavior affects the ecology, mindset, and emotions of our immediate environment.

These disciplines divulge that trauma hugely affects the area of the brain that struggles for existence. It also leads to physical changes, transforming the alarm system of the brain, a substantial increase in the stress-induced hormone, and alterations in the system that sieves substantial information from the irrelevant. A traumatized individual often practices the same odd thing; this is so because of the involuntary changes that have occurred in their brain owing to the trauma they had suffered.

Disassociation poses a big problem in trauma. There is a need for the incorporation of components that concerns the trauma so that the brain is conscious of what is present and what is past.

CHILDHOOD CONDITIONING

The place of a loving parental figure in the life of a child cannot be downplayed. It sets the tone for how they will connect with themselves, relate with others and the world they live in. Every child needs a guide, the duty of the parent figure to a child is to give them a secure base, where the child can always run back to after facing the challenges of the world and still feel safe.

A guide is not judgmental and leaves room for the child to exist just as they are, to make their mistakes, and also learn from them. The prerequisite to be a worthy parent figure in this context is evidence of the scars from your own healed and resolved trauma. The parent figure makes it a point of duty to make sure the child doesn't make the same mistakes they made and guides them aright.

A child that grew up lonely, shamed, rejected, lacking love, care and attention will most likely grow up dysfunctional because of the dearth of emotional care. It becomes worse as they grow into adulthood, this emotional loneliness is aggravated and becomes the worst of its kind. This is how trauma is passed on from one generation to the other through behaviors, habits, and beliefs that are imprinted unconsciously. We all know that children learn from what they see; they mimic the habits around them, the way to speak, diction, beliefs, coping mechanism, and more.

The work here is to intentionally observe your loved one and the bond you share just the same way witness you consciously. There are steps you must reach to help you to properly heal from all the buried pain, anger, sadness, hate, and depression; such as

- Come to a place where you know that identifying your wounding is a crucial step for the healing process.
- Old scars might need to be reopened so that each feeling is addressed and healing can properly take place.

To understand childhood trauma properly, these archetypes were developed by the author based on the common dynamics witnessed in her extensive clinical practice and inside the Self Healer community.

THE ARCHETYPES OF CHILDHOOD TRAUMA

- Having parents that deny your reality.
- Having parents that don't see or hear you.
- Having parents that vicariously live through you or molds and shapes you.
- Having parents that do not model boundaries.
- Having parents that are too fixated on physical appearance.
- Having parents who cannot control their emotions.

COPING WITH OUR TRAUMAS

A coping mechanism by two great psychologists – late UC Berkeley professor Richard Lazarus and UC San Francisco professor Susan Folkman in 1984 who studied stress and emotion defined it as "constantly changing cognitive behavior efforts to manage specific external and internal demands that [exceed] the resources of a person."

This goes to say that coping is a learned approach to help in managing the agitation in the mind and body that stress produces. Both psychologists outlined adaptive and maladaptive coping mechanisms.

Adaptive coping is the act of doing what we do to make us feel safe such as redirecting negative thoughts, the idea is to make sure you are not ideal; while maladaptive coping tactics, give temporary distraction from the discomfort. For example; drinking alcohol... But both of these methods take us far away from Self.

Our coping mechanism in a particular environment has little or nothing to do with the environment and much more to do with our accustomed coping strategies surrounding stress. Maladaptive coping tactics cannot be sustained, so it doesn't last; such as anger, dissociation, pleasing people, etc.

THE POTENTIAL FOR CHANGE

The truth is when we do the work right, we can heal. Realizing "Self" which is self-awareness is a big step in the right direction if we are to find solutions to trauma. It begins from the frontal part of the brain which comprises the medial prefrontal cortex, the orbital prefrontal cortex, the insula, the anterior cingulate, and the posterior cingulate. In the cases of severely traumatized people, they have successfully cut off that area in the brain (medial prefrontal activation) that makes them susceptible to feelings and emotions. This makes them live without drive, direction, and ultimately self-awareness.

- **Lessons**
1. Individuals suffering from trauma struggle to come to terms with what is going on in their bodies.

2. Trauma is not limited to the mind; it is expressed physiologically as well.
3. Children surpass us in their association to their intuition and their true Self.

- **Issues surrounding the subject matter**

1. Why do traumatized individuals have a hard time connecting with their emotions?

_____

_____

_____

_____

_____

_____

_____

_____

_____

- **Goals**

1. How can traumatized individuals assume control of their brains when imprisoned by their fight for survival?

_____

_____

_____

_____

_____

_____

_____

_____

_____

_____

2. How can the traumatized learn to live in the present if they keep dwelling in the past and how can they break free from this bondage?

_____

_____

_____

_____

_____

_____

_____

_____

3. How do we deal with the archetypes of childhood trauma?

_____

_____

_____

_____

_____

_____

_____

_____

- **Action steps**

1. To lessen the effect of a traumatic experience. Try to talk about it by reaching out to others that can help – it can be family or even a therapist.
2. Take medications that will put off pointless alarm responses or implement approaches that will make the brain process information right.
3. The traumatized should be flooded with experiences contradictory to their grief so that their brain is not always reverting to flight, flight, or total shutdown mode.

- **Checklist**

1. How you were treated as a child is not a reflection of who you are, who the mistreated is; nor are you a reflection of their unprocessed trauma.

CHAPTER 4: TRAUMA BODY

Nine out of every ten psychologically symptomatic patients have underlined physical health challenges. Unsolved trauma has a way of taking hold of our entire being. As ACEs rightly revealed about trauma and the psychological and physical conditions that erupt as a result, such as anxiety and depression resulting in cancer, heart attacks, stroke, obesity, and more. It is no longer news that individuals with trauma don't live long and are often sick.

Trauma affects the body in different and complex ways. A common denominator of physical dysfunction is stress. Many think that stress is just a mental state, but the truth is it is much more than that. Stress is an inner condition that threatens our emotional, physical, and mental balance which is homeostasis. Unresolved trauma triggers physiological stress reactions because the brain observes that it lacks enough resources to handle the threat. The addiction and stress expert who is also the author of various books as well as *When the Body Says No: The Cost of Hidden Stress* – Dr. Gabor Maté called this response the "stress-disease connection"

As humans, we cannot avoid stress, when our bodies are stressed (normative stress inclusive) the body swings into engaging all the resources available to protecting itself instead of helping to maintain homeostasis. Allostasis takes place because of the fluctuations of going back and forth from our baseline of balance. The body responds to stress with coping mechanisms such as fight or flight, flee and freeze.

Immediately the brain perceives danger, the amygdala lights up which is the center of the brain's fear, and the body is prompted that it is under attack and all the necessary details to aid survival is mobilized. In situations of severe stress, our adrenal glands dispense cortisol and other stress hormones unending like adrenaline.

One of the hormones vital to help fight/flee/freeze when faced with unfriendly situations is adrenaline. Increased heart rate and blood pressure are attributed to a sudden increase in adrenaline. For normal people when there is an increase in adrenaline due to events that call for the increase; after the danger is out of the way, the body system returns to the status quo. On the other hand, for traumatized people, very little things in the direction of the past increase their stress hormones and it takes too long to normalize.

The result of constantly increased stress hormones leads to bad temper, retention and attention complications, sleep disorders, and various lasting health issues. This stress also affected the physical body and not only the brain. As the muscles of the body stretch and stiffens whether, for fight or flight mode, it negatively affects various parts of the body organ.

Stress triggers the immune system of the body and prompts it to be highly vigilant and ready to act at the minutest suspicion of trouble. When the immune system constantly sends signals to the Brian of risk, this builds the fire starter chemicals that cause inflammation in the body leading to mental illness from depression and anxiety to downright psychosis. These chemicals reveal in symptoms like chronic pain, imbalance, dysfunction, increased chances of autoimmune diseases, cancer, and other heart diseases. An example of such inflammatory chemicals is cytokines. If the body's immune system keeps getting a constant release of such chemicals, then the body will fail to respond to the signs of authentic illness when the situation arises. Stress and trauma heavily hamper the immune system and brain which led to the new field of inquiry "mind-body connection" known as psychoneuroimmunology.

Another part of the body that stress significantly affects asides the brain is the gut. It affects the functionality of the gut, our food choices and hampers the proper breaking down the process of the food. No wonder most patients with anxiety suffer gastrointestinal (GI) issues. The body struggles to digest food when stressed or terrified, thereby leading to constipation or irritated/loose bowel (irritable bowel syndrome or diarrhea). All these lead to a sicker you.

The stress-disease connection is worse for oppressed populations such as BIPOC (Black, Indigenous, and people of color) that are always exposed to mental stress because of the constant discrimination and segregation from the supremacist system of governance. The records have it that BIPOC's have the highest rates of depression, physical illness, anxiety, psychological distress and more likely to develop lower back pain, hypertension, cancer, and artery calcifications.

These issues are often taken for granted but research has it that bigotry, racism, and bias get stored in the cells of the body and alters the body's entire functionality in destructive ways that pass from one generation to the other.

INTRODUCTION TO POLYVAGAL THEORY

Unresolved trauma plus bad coping mechanism hampers on the body physiologically and changes your reality.

Psychiatrist Dr. Stephen Porges brought about a groundbreaking revelation on trauma and how the body responds to stress, called a polyvagal theory. The theory revealed how trauma lives in the human body and how it forms our world.

The aforementioned term *"polyvagal"* speaks of the vagus nerve that connects the brain and the gut. The vagus nerve has numerous branches of sensory fibers running all through the entire body that connects every main organ to the brain.

The location and function of these nerves help one to know why the body acts fast when stressed, why our hearts skip beats when we run into an ex, why we run short of breath when we panic and why anyone will even pass out a time (faint). When we achieve homeostasis, there is a natural break caused by the vagus nerve to keep us calm and receptive. In cases when the vagus nerve is initiated and it goes to the defensive system, any of the coping mechanisms (fight-or-flight mode, flee, freeze) can manifest itself automatically.

SOCIAL ENGAGEMENT

To be almost constantly in fight-or-flight mode calls for an automatic function of the autonomic nervous system. This part of the nervous system is the one that regulates involuntary functions, breathing, heartbeat, and digestion.

The autonomic nervous system's job is to correctly allocate the body's resources and continuously scanning our environment for cues. The aforementioned makes use of "neuroception" which is the sixth sense to help in operating outside the confines of our conscious awareness to reach the environment and set people, things, and places as either safe or unsafe.

Some of the most common emotional and relational patterns of chronic stress include:

- Absence of emotional resilience
- Failure to form meaningful connections
- Challenges with concentration
- Trouble performing higher-functioning rational tasks, like planning for the future
- Concern delaying gratification

It is imperative to know that as humans, we switch to fight-or-flight mode completely involuntarily, we don't have a say in this. Another coping mechanism is the immobilization of freezing mode. A polyvagal-informed therapist – Justin Sunseri, describes immobilization mode using a bear in an illustration. He said if we see a bear, our mobilization mode may be activated, we may either flee or act dead (freeze).

THE SOCIAL WORLD

Also, there is social stress that manifests amongst others, you either feel uncomfortable at the sight of others or something about their existence threatens you. As interpersonal beings that require connection to survive, our dysregulated nervous system due to unanswered trauma has us unsatisfied, trapped in our incompetence to connect with others and outside our emotions.

CO-REGULATION

Like was outlined earlier, children are a product of what their parent figure poured into them. If they are groomed in a hostile environment filled with threats, then their nervous system will constantly release stress hormones so that the child feels a sense of safety from the supposed imminent danger.

On the other hand, when the sense of safety is passed on to others, it is called co-regulation. The cycle goes on and on like so – when we reassure others that there is no threat, they will also feel safe and enter the same social activation mode where everything is peaceful. On the other hand, when we are threatened and pass on that emotion to those around us, this makes all of us stuck thereby leading to emotional addiction.

EMOTIONAL ADDICTION

A loop of emotional addiction takes place when trauma is unresolved and it begins to dictate our narratives and form our autonomic responses. Then our body and mind begin to become dependent on the strong physical reaction coming from the discharge of neurotransmitters connected with that experience and coagulate it in the neural pathways of the brain. This is the way that the brain learns to desire the feelings connected with the trauma response.

In times when we encounter a powerful emotion, we either encounter activation or our immobilization mode is activated and we quickly go back to our baseline social engagement zone. An activation state is supposed to make one feel uneasy, unpleasant, and risky but those that are stuck in the loop of emotional addiction enjoy the rush it comes with.

Our body then tends to release hormones like cortisol and neurochemicals like dopamine which alters our cellular chemistry entirely. This makes those stuck in the emotional addiction loop seek a similar type of emotional nudge time and time again. This is similar to other addictions like sex, drug, sugar, alcohol, etc.

COMING FULL CIRCLE

This calls for an improvement of our vagal tone and nervous system responses to stop exaggerating its reactions or give faulty feedbacks and causing the body to release stress-related chemicals when there is no cause for alarm. The body needs to come to an understanding that it's not on constant attack and should stop the release of these hormones that causes inflammation, gut issues and does more harm than good to the body.

Doing the work means you have to tap into your nervous system dysregulation by witnessing yourself if not your body will experience symptoms such as psychological (*Activation symptoms, Shutdown symptoms*), physical (*Hypervigilance symptoms, Tension symptoms*), emotional (*social anxiety, irritability, social withdrawal*), social (*Attachment symptoms*)

- **Lessons**
1. Nine out of every ten psychologically symptomatic patients have underlined physical health challenges.
2. Trauma affects the body in different and complex ways and a common denominator of physical dysfunction is stress.
3. Stress is an inner condition that threatens our emotional, physical, and mental balance which is homeostasis.

4. Unresolved trauma triggers physiological stress reactions because the brain observes that it lacks enough resources to handle the perceived threat.

- **Issues surrounding the subject matter**

1. What is your understanding that stress is not just a mental state as it is much more than that?

_____

_____

_____

_____

_____

_____

_____

_____

_____

_____

- **Goals**

1. How do we restore balance to our nervous system?

_____

_____

_____

_____

_____

_____

_____

_____

_____

_____

2. Doing the work means we have to tap into our nervous system dysregulation by witnessing ourselves. How do you intend to carry that out and what are the benefits to gain from this process?

_____

_____

_____

_____

_____

_____

_____

_____

_____

- **Action steps**
1. Restore balance to your nervous system by finding your ground in the present moment (be self-aware), engage in visualization meditation, pay attention to how you consume information and find nature and witness it.
- **Checklist**
1. Restoring balance to your nervous system requires consistency no matter how little the efforts are, continue and it will take effect soon.

CHAPTER 5: MIND-BODY HEALING PRACTICES

The revelation gained from the nervous system and polyvagal theory helped the author to get rid of shame. She discovered that all the parts of herself she wrestled with had a physiological foundation. They happened to be the oversensitive impulses of her dysregulated body. To make matters worse, those habits and behaviors (survival mechanisms) are part of the reasons why she still lives regardless of how ill they may be.

Our bodies learn dysregulated coping mechanism; so it is also able to learn healthy pathways to recovery. Recall that epigenetics revealed that our genes aren't fixed owing to neuroplasticity which helps to form new pathways with the assistance of the brain, our conscious mind helps us recognize the strength of our thoughts to make change happen, and with the polyvagal theory, we know how the nervous system affects other parts of the body.

As we come into a realization of witnessing Self, we get the potential to heal. This helps us to unlearn and relearn all that puts us in harm's way. We can tap into the power that enables our bodies to heal our minds and our minds to heal our bodies. Paying attention to Self and getting physically active can give your body a total turnaround. It can increase your capacity for endurance in terms of discomfort and stress. It also positively affects your diet thereby reducing inflammation and corrects autoimmune disorders in the body.

TOP-DOWN, BOTTOM-UP (BODY-TO-BRAIN AND BRAIN-TO-BODY CONVERSATION)

Healing can only begin when you know how to reach the needs of your body and reconnect with your intuitive Self. Below are the steps to total healing;

1. Witness yourself – listen to your body's responses. This will help to activate the vagus nerve to help in balancing the nervous system.

2. Engage in physical exercises such as meditation and yoga – meditation helps in regulating the responses of your autonomic nervous system, yoga helps to strengthen our musculoskeletal and cardiovascular systems, reduce the sympathetic responses in our nervous system and decrease psychological stress. Aside from yoga, other polyvagal nerves (bottom-up) engaging exercises are cold therapy, breath work, etc.

All of these are important tools for strengthening the mind-body connection and promoting a healthy vagal tone. They are the introductory steps to holistic healing.

HEALING THE GUT

Many people complain about uncomfortable digestive issues and complex feelings about food and mostly live their lives with severe gut and digestive concerns. For these clients, it is helpful to gain an awareness of the effects of their nutrition on their body and thus their mental state. Many also indulge in emotional eating, be it out of obligation, a habit, or out of necessity. It is common practice not to eat based on the nutrition that the body needs to survive but based on how we feel then.

As we advance in age, we stop listening to those innate reasons to eat healthy due to various changes that have affected our brain so far and so we react based on various kinds of stress levels. Our gut is like an abode to a broad network of nerve cells along the gut wall that makes up the enteric nervous system (ENS). This is a mesh-like system of nerve cells that is quite multifaceted often called "second brain."

In a traumatized state, the presence of any physical dysregulation in the nervous system and the gut hinders proper food digestion to take place nor the proper absorption of the nutrients to be benefited by the body. In a stressed-out state, our body cannot assume the normal parasympathetic state responsible for sending messages of security and peace to the body. This results in symptoms like constipation n diarrhea because our body cannot expel or hold on to the food been taken it. After a while, our body becomes starved of important nutrients needed to make us healthy no matter the quantity of food and frequency in which we decide to eat.

Not only do we become malnourished, but our intestinal lining gets inflamed for the unhealthy choices of food we take in like processed carbohydrates, sugar, and inflammatory fats (such as trans fats and many vegetable oils). This particular situation allows an uneven balance of the inner ecosystem to favor the "bad" bugs which is a condition known as gut dysbiosis. Gut Dysbiosis causes leaky guts that allow bacteria into the circulatory system of the body. This can lead to major inflammation and even cause us to feel lethargic, sick, or even psychologically ill. Gut Dysbiosis is also said to be responsible for autism, ADHD, mental illness, depression, and schizophrenia.

RESTORING THE INTEGRITY OF THE GUT

The good news is that the integrity of the gut wall can be restored with the aid of a healthy diet (eating whole, nutrient-dense foods, also fermented foods such as yogurt, sauerkraut, kimchi, and kefir which are naturally rich in probiotics) alongside supplementary probiotics, and then even positively affect your mental health by alleviating its symptoms.

Another nutritional approach supported by many academic studies to regain the gut's health is engaging in intermittent fasting. This gives your digestive system a healthy break and benefits your vagal tone. Also, your insulin sensitivity rises, and your blood sugar is regulated. Intermittent fasting increases mental awareness, alertness, and learning.

Other practices that help our body and mind heal properly is undergoing the following;

- **Healing sleep** – sleep is crucial to our mental and physical health. Inadequate sleep is detrimental to the body. Sleep time is the time the body gets to repair itself, it shouldn't be negotiable.
- **Healing with breath** - Doing breath-work engages the autonomic nervous system. Using our breath to soothe our arousal system allows us to communicate with the brain that our environment is void of threatening and the message is passed to the entire body. There are various breath-work techniques, go with the one you prefer.
- **Healing with movement** – the place of physical activity cannot be overemphasized. It helps to expand our horizon and gives a clearer view to better understand Self and your intuition. Exercises alleviate your mood, help you sleep better, relieve stress, reduces inflammation levels, and regulates blood pressure.
- **Healing with play** – having some fun when we can is good for the entire well-being of the body. Sheer joy is priceless, even the thoughts of treasured moments make you blush all over again. Joy heals, it's great for you. Do the things you love, go see a movie with friends, go to the beach and bath in the sun, just be happy.

We have all it takes to gain absolute control over our consciousness and the transformational power to change the mind. It involves understanding you we were in time past, meet our inner child, fall in love with our ego, and continue to learn of the traumatic bonds that keep shaping our world.

- **Lessons**
1. Healing can only begin when you know how to reach the needs of your body and reconnect with your intuitive Self.
2. Gut Dysbiosis causes leaky guts that allow bacteria into the circulatory system of the body. This can lead to major inflammation and even cause us to feel lethargic, sick, or even psychologically ill.

- **Issues surrounding the subject matter**
1. How can we reach inwards to seek out what the body needs and reconnect with our intuitive self for healing to begin?

_____

_____

_____

_____

_____

_____

_____

_____

_____

_____

- **Goals**

1. How do you plan to heal yourself using, breathwork, play, movement, and sleep?

_____

_____

_____

_____

_____

_____

_____

_____

_____

_____

_____

_____

_____

_____

_____

_____

_____

2. In what ways are you going to restore the integrity of your gut?

_____

_____

_____

_____

_____

_____

_____

_____

_____

_____

- **Action steps**
1. Write down the breathwork you have chosen to do daily to aid a smooth holistic healing process.

_____

_____

_____

_____

_____

_____

_____

_____

_____

_____

_____

_____

_____

_____

_____

_____

_____

_____

_____

- **Checklist**
1. In working on toning your vagus nerve, it is notable to note that you will certainly experience painful internal pushback.

CHAPTER 6: THE POWER OF BELIEF

We often tell ourselves things just so that we can do right by ourselves and survive. All it takes is for us to believe what we have said, then whatever story has been told receives power and can drive you for long. Based on our developmental age as children, we are confined by what we can emotionally and cognitively understand. So we blame ourselves and think we are bad when our parent figure hits us, whereas it is the parent figure who finds it hard to manage their rage. From our tender age, we are wired for survival and the most indelible and significant imprints are often culled from those we bond mostly with – our parent figures.

As humans, we are led to tell ourselves alleviating stories so that we can keep living even as we hurt badly. What our reality holds is so painful to come to terms with, so we think up an alternative story to keep us sane and alive. This is peculiar with neglected children; they make up stories so they seem perfect before their peers. Many of us grow up making various narratives to survive the harsh realities of the world and still are as we speak. We make up a narrative about ourselves, about others, about the world, about our future, and many more.

THE ORIGIN OF BELIEF

A belief is a rehearsed thought built on experienced happenings. Beliefs are built up after many years of thought patterns which entails both interior and exterior validation before they can thrive. Our beliefs reveal how we view the world. The more practice we give to particular thoughts, the more likely for them to become real as the brain wires itself to make these thought patterns the default setting, especially if the thoughts stimulate our stress response and vagus nerve. Throughout consistent repetition of thought patterns, it becomes compulsive.

Beliefs that are continually validated, become a core belief. Core beliefs are our deepest opinions about our identity; they are often ingrained in our subconscious before we are seven years old. Immediately we form a core belief, make sure to carry out a confirmation of bias. This will eliminate the information that doesn't go in line with your beliefs and replaced it with the information that does.

Try to concentrate on things in our environment that are of benefit to you. This is the job of the reticular activating system (RAS). This subconscious filters using a group of nerves in the brain stem that helps us sort out our immediate environment and lets us concentrate on what is essential.

Our RAS can either benefit us positively or negatively. It can be used as a lens to see how negative the world is to you and can be equally used as a defense mechanism to tell yourself that the world holds some good despite the contrary vibes you are getting.

CHILDHOOD INTERRUPTED

As the brain matures, the basic needs of every human which are food, shelter, and love widen to a more complicated need for emotional, physical, and spiritual satisfaction such as a strong desire to be heard, to be seen, and to express our true selves.

Many children have their childhood snatched from them when they are forced to be less sensitive, whereas all they are craving is love which is perceived as weakness. In a bid not to be seen as such, they toughen up, lock away their emotions, detached, withdrawn, and grows up into a dysfunctional adult whose core belief is void of his/her authentic Self. Growing up, we are then made to envision the world through those core beliefs we made up from negative experiences in childhood.

Beliefs are powerful tools to reconstruct your present and even future. Our subconscious mind can be shaped and reshaped by thoughts, it only requires dedication and perseverance and in no time it will be.

- **Lessons**
1. Beliefs are practiced thoughts and creating a new belief requires practicing a new thought.
2. From our tender age, we are wired for survival and the most indelible and significant imprints are often culled from those we bond mostly with – our parent figures.

3. Beliefs that are continually validated, become a core belief.

- **Issues surrounding the subject matter**

1. How can an individual who has practically had the worse childhood reach out to learn new positive beliefs?

_____

_____

_____

_____

_____

_____

_____

_____

_____

- **Goals**

1. Share the stories you have ever told yourself and forced yourself to believe it just to help you survive and how it turned out.

_____

_____

_____

_____

_____

_____

_____

_____

_____

_____

_____

_____

_____

_____

_____

_____

_____

2. How can you create a new belief?

_____

_____

_____

_____

_____

_____

_____

_____

- **Action steps**
1. Make a belief inventory by spending ample time to reflect on and take actual notes of your core beliefs –

for yourself, the world around you, others, the future, and other topics of great concern to you. Pick one per time you will begin to change and how you intend to go about it.

_____

_____

_____

_____

_____

_____

_____

_____

_____

_____

_____

_____

_____

_____

_____

_____

_____

_____

_____

_____

_____

- **Checklist**
1. At the onset, you may find it hard to believe the new thought of yourself but keep practicing. Soon your brain will convince you that all that you are saying can come true.

CHAPTER 7: MEET YOUR INNER CHILD

Every one of us holds an inner child within us, the situations that arise from growing up heavily affect how our inner child will turn out to be.

ATTACHMENT THEORY

The contents of our earliest childhood bonds cannot be overemphasized. Simply put, the kind of relationship we have with our parent figure serves as a bedrock for the kind of relationships we will be open to having as adults. This sort of relationship is called attachments.

In 1952 Psychoanalyst; John Bowlby brought a theory of attachment after his study on children and the relationship they share with their mothers at a clinic in London. Children live for the attention; they crave it with every fiber in their being. Children exhibit various social releasers like smiling crying and more just to get the attention of their parent figures. John Bowlby concluded that all of this extreme display is driven by their instinct to survive.

Bowlby's work was continued by the developmental psychologist Mary Ainsworth who created the Strange Situation Classifications. The practice evaluated diverse attachment styles by taking note of a child's response when the mother is absent and when she returns.

Ainsworth's observation and study outlined four diverse attachment styles during the first eighteen months of a child's life. They are;

- **Secure** – a receptive child who has experienced a quantifiable amount of tender love and care.
- **Anxious-resistant** – this infant is mostly distressed and stressed out from his mother's absence, upon the parent's return the child refuses to be comforted thereby displaying misattunement.
- **Anxious** – infants in this category don't react to stress when their parent leaves or returns, they avoid their parents and this is a product of disconnected parent-figure.
- **Disorganized-disoriented** – infants in this category don't display a predictable pattern of response. They are erratic and can display any emotion at any time. In the four attachment styles, this is the rarest and it is associated with the childhood traumas discovered on the ACEs, such as severe abuse and neglect.
  Numerous other factors are attributing to the upbringing that is responsible for the insanity experienced by traumatized persons; such as the lag in motherly care especially for men taken early from their mother's arms responsible for their misconduct. Separating an infant from its parent-figure/mother will negatively affect the child's psyche and in the long run, hinders the discovery of "Self".

As social beings, we seek to be among a homogenous community actively impacting each other. We begin to learn from the time of birth, with every care we get, we learn ways to dote on ourselves and care for others. A peaceful and loving home will often groom a self-reliant, confident and emphatic child.

INTRODUCING THE INNER CHILD

Everyone has an inner child within, our reactions to issues of life reveal how dysfunctional/traumatic, or receptive our inner child was groomed to be. Our inner child can only be accessed on the condition that we safely connect to the social connection zone of our nervous system, become open and spontaneous again. No wonder many adults grow up today with so much they are holding back, scared of being loved and expressing love.

Most adults walking around today are carrying deep inner child injuries caused by a repetition of unmet physical, emotional, and spiritual needs from infancy conveyed through our subconscious and still calls the shots even our adulthood.

Here are 7 inner child archetypes created by those unmet needs;

1. **The hero worshipper**- the inner child craves to follow a person and lives modeling after others.

2. **The overachiever**- the inner child sees success and achievement as the true worth or value and nothing more.
3. **The caretaker**- the inner child neglects its core needs just to gain a sense of identity and self-worth.
4. **The life of the party**- the inner child constantly seeks to make those around them happy in a bid to conceal the emotions they are ashamed of.
5. **The underachiever** – they stay away from the faces of people in other not to be criticized or termed a failure.
6. **The yes-person**- nothing else matters than serving others.
7. **The rescuer/protector** – saves those around to cover up their vulnerability.

The bottom line here is to work at personalizing and incorporating the feeling that you are good enough, more than enough, and don't need the approval to believe that you are worthy.

- **Lessons**
1. Coming to terms with your inner child will help you eradicate the shame and disappointment in your pathway to change.
2. Our inner child can only be accessed on the condition that we safely connect to the social connection zone of our nervous system, become open and spontaneous again.

- **Issues surrounding the subject matter**
1. How do we personalize and incorporate the feeling that we are good enough and worthy of love?

_____

_____

_____

_____

_____

_____

_____

_____

- **Goals**
1. In what ways do you intend to spend time reflecting and witnessing your inner child?

_____

_____

_____

_____

_____

_____

_____

_____

_____

2. List out the things you aim to reflect on and witness about your inner child. (outlining them all will give you a broader prospect on ways to address them)

_____

_____

_____

_____

_____

_____

_____

_____

_____

_____

_____

_____

_____

_____

_____

_____

_____

_____

- **Action steps**
1. Write an inner child letter to you using the archetype(s) that best describes you.

_____

_____

_____

_____

_____

_____

_____

_____

_____

_____

_____

_____

_____

_____

_____

_____

_____

_____

_____

2. Get an inner child guided meditation from a reliable source.

- **Checklist**

1. The situations that arise from growing up heavily affect how our inner child will turn out.

CHAPTER 8: EGO STORIES

MEET THE EGO

We can rightly conclude that our ego heavily impacts and drives our core belief of Self. With this knowledge in mind, how our ego drives our mannerism is void of us. The ego is the esteemed protector of our inner child which happens to be our "I" identity. The words we say that come after "I" are an extension of our ego – *I'm good. I'm bad. I'm beautiful. I'm ugly...*

Our ego serves as our personality, sense of self, and self-worth. Our ego is an astute narrator that creates and maintains certain narratives about what we believe about ourselves. Our ego belief is imbibed from lived experiences from our parent figures, relatives, friends, our community, and our society at large. Our ego has a strong influence on us, it interprets our thoughts and entire belief system to reveal our deepest fear or courage.

EGO ACTIVATION

Our ego is extremely alert and never lets its guard off at protecting you. It is often aggressive to oppositions, never wanting to compromise or be compassionate, and is very rigid. The ego is always ready to defend and act when it perceives any form of opposition. Threats against our ego Self can show in the ensuing ways:

1. Displaying strong emotional reactivity

2. Displaying false confidence
3. Displaying lack of nuance in thinking
4. Displaying extreme competition

These are the reactions displayed when there is a synthesis among your beliefs, opinions, selfhood, and thoughts. Ego makes everything in the world about you and what you believe, anything opposing them both is a threat.

With ego, the goal is to stamp your worth and power and doesn't have time to get familiar with or agree on a shared truth. That's what happens when mild differences turn ugly, that's a show of childhood injuries and activation dragged along from childhood.

EGO PROJECTIONS

In life, we don't have to know anything about the stranger right in front of us but our ego projection is good at cooking up a story and frames it in line with our past experiences without even exchanging words with the stranger. Ego stories come easily to us, as humans; the mind is frightened by uncertainty, it's just part of being humans.

HOW TO DO THE WORK WITH YOUR EGO

The ego work entails being aware and conscious in place of complying with our ego's response to our world. The ego work also entails witnessing. When we are on autopilot, our ego takes control and does as it pleases, but engaging the conscious mind aids our ego to loosen its grip on our lives.

Here are the steps to get the best out of our ego;

Step 1- let your ego introduce itself (you are separate from your ego; so practice being a neutral witness)

Step 2- have a friendly meeting with your ego (intentionally take note of your thought pattern and what comes after when you use the words "I am". Try to take mental notes or write them down, don't be judgmental, don't exasperate or feel disappointed. This will help you to know the contents of your emotions all day long, whether they are negative or positive. Once that is known, start repeating only the positives to yourself as that will open up new pathways in the brain to allow witnessing to find expression)

Step 3- give your ego a name (this will help you separate from it. Disentangling our intuitive Self from our ego is possible if we can successfully give it a name)

Meet activated ego- being consciously aware makes us separate from our ego stories. Our thoughts aren't who we are, we can't stop our thoughts from coming.

- **Lessons**
1. Our ego serves as our personality, sense of self, and self-worth.
2. Our ego belief is imbibed from lived experiences from our parent figures, relatives, friends, our community, and our society at large.
3. The ego work entails being aware, conscious, and self-witnessing.

- **Issues surrounding the subject matter**

1. Why do you avoid talking about your emotions?
2. What are the negative words that come with the phrase "I am"?
- **Goals**
1. What are the ways you will begin to be more open about discussing your emotions?

_____

_____

_____

_____

_____

_____

_____

_____

_____

2. How can you stop your negative thought pattern?

_____

_____

_____

_____

_____

_____

_____

_____

_____

3. How can you change your ego consciousness to empower consciousness?

_____

_____

_____

_____

_____

_____

_____

_____

_____

- **Action steps**
1. To be empowered to break out of your ego's accustomed habits and patterns, start to make adequate room to help you not to return to your older ego reactions. Practice breaking away from the old habit of emotional reactivity by your daily choices. Be more aware of your activities, try not to stay on autopilot for too long.
2. Meet your shadow self and take time out to reflect deeply on why you act the way you do when a certain situation arises.

- **Checklist**
1. How you speak about yourself to others shows your self-narratives and the beliefs that limit you.

CHAPTER 9: TRAUMA BONDS

Dr. Patrick Carnes; author of *The Betrayal Bond: Breaking Free of Exploitive Relationships* research coined the term *"traumatic bonding."* This term describes the relationship between two people with self-doubting attachment. In other words, this talks about a problematic bond that is fortified by neurochemical expressions of reward (love) and punishment (removal of love). The most extreme case of traumatic bonding as revealed by Dr. Carnes which he focused on are;

1. Domestic violence
2. Child abuse
3. Incest
4. Stockholm syndrome cases of, cults, kidnappings, and hostage-taking.

Dr. Carnes explained traumatic bond as the act of seeking comfort from the hands of the source of their trauma. It can be the person who abuses and hurts them or an addiction that they keep returning to and doing things that hurt their very being, but they seem to have a supposed inseparable bond with this sweet poison.

What the traumatized person has successfully done is to get the best coping mechanism and entangle themselves in that evil bond. This phenomenon is just sheer misuse of fear, sexual feelings, excitement, and sexual physiology to enslave another individual. The relationship pattern of the trauma bond keeps you trapped in things that don't allow you to express your true self. Trauma bonds are learned and shaped from childhood and carried all the to adulthood. These behaviors affected by trauma bonds show up in our romantic relationships, peer relationships, family relationships, and even professionally.

Trauma bonds reveal what our deepest spiritual, physical, and emotional needs are. Here are some common signs you will observe in a trauma bond:

- Having an obsessive and compulsive appeal towards certain kinds of relationships even though you are aware it is detrimental.
- Not knowing what your needs are in the relationship or not having your needs met at all & still choose to stay.
- Betraying yourself by staying in a certain relationship just to get your needs met with a connected lack of Self-trust.

The bottom line is that the body and mind crave love and once this is provided then an authentic bond is created, bond equals survival, and love equals life. When there is a drought of love and attention, it results in addiction, shame, and trauma bonds. When stress responses are seen as our homeostatic abode by the subconscious, we tend to confuse signs of threat & stress as sexual charm and chemistry. To make matters worse, we then develop a lethal addiction and get stuck in similar kinds of relationships of this sort for a very long time. The good news is that trauma bonding can be unlearned, it only takes dedication and time for it to work.

TRAUMA BOND ARCHETYPES

Witnessing your trauma is the first step to breaking trauma bond patterns. Take out time and go back in time to inquire of yourself what happened to you in the past, how did you get hurt, what really hurt you and how do you cope in your relationship now... these archetypes still apply

- Do you have parents who deny your reality?
- Do you have parents who do not see or hear you?
- Do you have parents who vicariously live through you or shapes you?
- Do you have parents who do not model boundaries?
- Do you have parents who are obsessively focused on appearance?
- Do you have parents who cannot control their emotions?

When our needs are ignored consistently, this brings about resentment, which is the whole essence of the trauma bond dynamic. When needs are consistently unmet, resentment soon follows.

AUTHENTIC LOVE

Trauma bonds don't mean your relationship is doomed. They serve as teachers and helps to earmark the areas in your life you should work on improving. Relationships will only thrive if it is not used as a means to fill the vacuum or injuries inflicted by the parent figure.

A healthy relationship gives room for mutual evolution. The essence of authentic love is having two people allow each other the liberty and support to be fully heard, seen, and Self-expressed.
Building authentic love needs work. The way forward is becoming aware of the part you play in self-betrayal in your trauma bonds and the part you can play in respecting your own needs.

- **Lessons**
1. Resentment kills relationships.
- **Issues surrounding the subject matter**
1. Why does a traumatic bond have to do with seeking comfort in the hands of our oppressors?

_____

_____

_____

_____

_____

_____

_____

- **Goals**
1. List out all the ways you deny your emotions and live a life of deceit and why?

_____

_____

_____

_____

_____

_____

_____

_____

_____

_____

_____

_____

_____

_____

_____

_____

_____

_____

_____

2. Do you have parent figures that are excessively focused on appearance? If yes, try to spend time witnessing yourself, don't go judging or criticizing your relationship with your physical appearance. Guide your witnessing by providing answers to these question adequately;

- How do I speak about other people's physical appearance?

_____

_____

_____

_____

_____

_____

- How do I speak to my friends about my body?

_____

_____

_____

_____

_____

_____

_____

_____

- How do I speak to myself about my body?

_____

_____

_____

_____

_____

_____

_____

_____

_____

- How often do I compare myself to other people physically?

_____

_____

3. Do you have parent figures who don't model boundaries? If yes, take out time to witness yourself, don't go judging or criticizing your relationship with your family, friends, romantic partners, etc. Guide your witnessing by providing answers to these question adequately;

- Are you open to saying "no" or do you feel guilty or scared to do so and why?

_____

_____

_____

_____

_____

_____

_____

_____

- Are you open to declare your limitations and your core feelings of situations and why?

_____

_____

_____

_____

_____

_____

_____

_____

- Are you the one to involuntarily force people to take your perspectives or views?

_____

_____

_____

_____

_____

_____

_____

_____

4. Do you have a parent figure that denies your reality, does not see or hear you, and vicariously lives through you or shapes you? if yes, do the following;

-   Reflect on and take notes down of how you respond when your thoughts, experiences, and feelings are denied by someone.

- Take time out to know the kind of experiences that triggers these feelings and note down your reactions
- Witness the events that occur which makes you feel unacknowledged.
- Note down the reasons that make you seek validation, want to be seen or heard.

- **Action steps**
1. If you had a parent figure that finds it hard to control their emotions; take some time out to witness how you control your own emotions now as an adult.
2. Spend some time noting down the several ways you continually deny some emotions repeatedly daily and several other areas of your life. Guide your reflections using these prompts and respond adequately;

- In a solid emotional experience, how do you respond?

_____

_____

_____

_____

_____

_____

_____

_____

_____

- What is the coping strategy you use when you feel stressed emotionally and why?

_____

_____

_____

_____

_____

_____

_____

_____

_____

- In a strong emotional experience, how do you connect with the people around you?

_____

_____

_____

_____

_____

_____

_____

_____

- After a strong emotional episode, do you swing into self-care or you withdraw into your shell and begin self-shaming yourself and why?

_____

_____

_____

_____

_____

_____

_____

_____

_____

_____

3. Note down how you experience and cope with your emotions.

- **Checklist**

1. Never forget, keep practicing these positive thought patterns. It may take time to kick in, but with time, you will become confident and comfortable in dealing with your limitations and vulnerabilities.

CHAPTER 10: BOUNDARIES

ENMESHMENT

Boundaries are important in life to help separate you (your needs, thoughts, emotions, beliefs, emotional and physical spaces) from others and help in developing and maintaining authentic connections. Setting boundaries and sticking to them is crucial for your state of mind. As a child, while growing up, if it was a struggle to set boundaries, it will show in your life as an adult. Not being able to set boundaries limits you from expressing your true Self.

Enmeshment is when in a family, boundaries are not respected and adhered to, the result is the fading out of emotional lines as no one in the family has the liberty to express their true Self. An enmeshed state is a sheer drought of separateness. Enmeshment is displayed by parent figures in the following ways;

- The excessive investment into their children's lives.
- Activating strong emotion across the entire family.
- Seriously frowning at family members who are spending time away from others in the family.
- The fear of not being able to control the child and the child having fears of being ostracized from the family.

The authentic connection doesn't exist because of a close bond, authentic connection is built on mutual sharing with clear-cut boundaries and the liberty to explore our separate realities all at once.

AN INTRODUCTION TO BOUNDARIES

Boundaries safeguards and defends you from what is unacceptable, inappropriate, and inauthentic. Boundaries keep you connected to your intuitive self and make sure you experience authentic love. With boundaries, we are more confident to express our true wants and needs, able to control our autonomic nervous system response better, and free ourselves of the hate that comes with refusing to admit to our essential needs.

Barriers to boundary work;

1. Niceness – living to please others and equating it for love or likeness in return. Learning to say no and in total control of your emotions expresses your true value. It has nothing to do with arrogance, it is knowing what you want, your limits, and the best way to communicate it.

2. Too-rigid boundaries- we leave no room for interconnectedness, flag strict rules of conduct and behavior for trespassers and prospective trespassers to be warned.

We all experience various forms of extreme as it concerns boundaries such as; rigid, flexible, and loose.

Boundaries are not for others but you. It is a personal limit expressed to drive your need to be met. In setting boundaries, it is imperative to allow others to have their limits and respect them while maintaining yours.

TYPES OF BOUNDARIES

1. *Physical boundary*- finding worth only in your appearance, how sexy you look, and what your body can do.
2. *Resource boundary*- finding Self-worth in constant giving in a bid to receive love.
3. *Mental/emotional boundary*- this is common in families with enmeshment challenges. We feel responsible for the loose mental/emotional boundaries and often swing into action to save the day.

Mental/emotional boundaries enable us to separate ourselves and our emotional world while allowing others to have their separate emotional world. With boundaries in place, we can more easily access our intuitive voice and better regulate our emotional states.

We all should aspire to be in a place of emotional safety where we are more relaxed to share our opinions, thoughts, opinions, and beliefs with others. We are not unnecessarily obliged to please others at all times.

EMOTIONAL DUMPING AND OVERSHARING

Emotional oversharing is a challenge common with the Self Healers community. A lot of us were encouraged to always share our feelings, most especially for those with enmeshed and intrusive parent-figures who stopped at nothing to demand full closure, encouraged oversharing, or divulged too much information at an inappropriate time; especially at a progressive stage when it isn't advised. Lack of boundaries causes more harm than good, yes there is a place and season in a man's life to be open, but it cannot be all through their lives.

The ability to choose is empowering to a large extent. The choice is key; it tells how much you have mastered and understood your thoughts, emotional state, and beliefs and that you own them and have the prerogative to share or not to share.

On the other hand, emotional dumping is when we spill emotional challenges on an individual short of empathy or concern for their emotional state. Emotional dumping is a coping skill intuitive of boundarylessness. This coping mechanism is often used to evade emotions we cannot handle. This mental/emotional boundary can be beneficial if both parties' feelings are mutually represented here.

HOW TO SET BOUNDARIES

Define the boundaries and search within to know the areas in your life lacking boundaries. Know what needs to shift or change in your life in other to help you feel more secure and safe in your relationships. The idea is to retrieve your stolen energy and everything that would make you happy, safe and comfortable.

Take out time to review your relationships, identify and outline your regular crossed boundaries (types such as; physical, mental/emotional, resource, etc.) This will guide you on where to begin to set your boundaries and set them right.

Another concern in doing the work is, don't be scared not to meet people's expectations of you. That's not to say that you will go about your life caring less about what others think of you. The moral here is not to tie your happiness and growth on the fulfillment of what others think are the expectations you own them.

Instead of expectations, give them a choice and if they behave in a manner that you don't like, the individual will face the same boundary tenets. The expectation is a two-way thing, understanding the limitation of others, seeing their pain, and witnessing their fear where cruelty once laid, then healing has taken place.

To do the work; Create a new boundary and do the following;

- Define the boundary – physical boundaries, mental-emotional boundaries, resource boundaries.
- Set boundary – communicate the new boundary and keep practicing consistently to effect the change.
- Maintain the boundary – don't go back to your old ways, hold on to your new boundary.

- **Lessons**
1. Boundaries connect us to our intuitive voice.
2. Boundaries are important in life to help separate you (your needs, thoughts, emotions, beliefs, emotional and physical spaces) from others and help in developing and maintaining authentic connections.
3. Setting boundaries and sticking to them is crucial for your state of mind.
- **Issues surrounding the subject matter**
1. What is the way we can set boundaries and stick to them unwavering?

_____

_____

_____

_____

_____

_____

_____

_____

_____

_____

- **Goals**
1. What can be done to make sure your needs are better met?

_____

_____

_____

_____

_____

_____

_____

_____

_____

_____

2. What do you need to change in your life or what aspect of your life needs to shift to make you feel safe and secure in your relationships?

_____

_____

_____

_____

_____

_____

_____

_____

_____

- **Action steps**
1. Create a new boundary using the following;
- Define the boundary – physical boundaries, mental-emotional boundaries, resource boundaries.
- Set boundary – communicate the new boundary and keep practicing consistently to effect the change.

- Maintain the boundary – don't go back to your old ways, hold on to your new boundary.
- **Checklist**

1. Not being able to set boundaries limits you from expressing your true Self.

CHAPTER 11: REPARENTING

Awakenings aren't often prompt like most people expect them to be. These things take time to manifest, if the result shows prematurely, then it will not last.

Psychologist Dr. Steve Taylor studied the phenomenon termed "awakenings". He calls them flashes of insight and realizations. Dr. Steve discovered that the awakening experiences have three common elements which are;

- They often emerge from a state of inner turmoil
- They often occur in a natural setting.
- They often connect us to some kind of spiritual practice.

Awakenings make it known that we are more than simple creations of flesh, that we have a soul that longs for connection to something greater than ourselves. Awakenings reveal that who we think we are doesn't tell us that that's who we are. The time and period in which your awakening shows up and lasts are peculiar to each one of us.

Your awakening period is not a fun time at all, it entails understanding your physical, emotional, and spiritual needs. It also entails ridding yourself of the old Self and becoming aware of yourself in ways that you have never.

AN INTRODUCTION TO REPARENTING

A child can only develop healthily if his/her basic needs are met. In infancy, when we are in need, we depend on our parent figure and the entire family unit to cater to our physical, spiritual, and emotional needs. It is the desire and cravings of a child to be seen, heard, held, and allowed to be their authentic Self. When our parent figure shows us support, we can learn how safe and liberal it is to express our deepest needs without been shot out and shunned. This kind of support and recognition builds the courage, self-esteem, and confidence of the child. On the other hand, if a parent figure is an emotionally immature one, the needs of the child will be unmet or not even attempted at all.

Emotional immaturity comes from a drought of emotional resilience, the capacity to process emotions, confer boundaries, and bring our nervous system back to balance. More attributes of an emotionally immature parent figure throw tantrums, act defensively or selfishly, and makes the entire family unit revolve around them.

The process of reparenting is going ahead with the awareness that you are now that wise parent to yourself that you didn't have while growing up. This way you have to unlearn all you knew about parenting your inner child and relearn how you will meet the unmet desires of your inner child by conscious actions and core dedication.

THE FOUR PILLARS OF REPARENTING

1. Emotional regulation, or the ability to successfully navigate our emotional states.
2. Loving discipline. We need to create boundaries with ourselves and maintain them over time. To make this happen, we are to be dedicated and resilient enough to make promises, develop daily routines and habits. Loving discipline promotes routine with empathy and flexibility.
3. Loving discipline: Self-care. Authentic self-care includes supporting your needs and treasuring your worth. It is not indulgent and it's basically for holistic wellness.
4. Relive our childlike sense of wonder. This state is made up of a blend of creativity, joy, imagination, playfulness, and spontaneity.

- **Lessons**

1. Reparenting entails unlearning all you knew about parenting your inner child and relearn how you will meet the unmet desires of your inner child by conscious actions and core dedication.
2. Discipline is a core part of the general healing process and nurturing it helps you to show up for yourself.
3. Parenting is not a walk in the park but it is amazingly emotionally activating.

- **Issues surrounding the subject matter**

1. Your awakening period is not a fun time, it entails understanding your physical, emotional, and spiritual needs. How can you go understanding these?

_____

_____

_____

_____

_____

_____

_____

_____

_____

- **Goals**
1. What are the tools needed to help you to successfully unlearn all you knew about parenting your inner child and relearn how you will meet the unmet desires of your inner child by conscious actions and core dedication?

_____

_____

_____

_____

_____

_____

_____

_____

_____

_____

_____

_____

_____

_____

_____

_____

_____

_____

_____

2. What role does discipline play in our holistic healing?

- **Action steps**

1. Doing the work entails developing a reparenting menu; using the above four pillars of reparenting, make the changes you desire to make to each.

- **Checklist**

1. Awakenings reveals that who we think we are doesn't mean that's who we are.

CHAPTER 12: EMOTIONAL MATURITY

Emotional maturity is nothing about our numerical age. Many of us were more mature than our parent figures even as teens. Emotional immaturity is the incapability to tolerate. Emotional immature folks display discomfort with their emotions and become defensive or shut down entirely.

Emotionally immature people are so uncomfortable with their emotions that they typically lash out and become defensive or completely shut down whenever they experience one. Still focused on parenting, Psychotherapist Lindsay Gibson says emotional is the "lack of emotional responsiveness necessary to meet children's emotional needs." The result for children of emotionally immature parent-figures is loneliness, emptiness – they feel they are alone in this world.

The feeling of emptiness often streams from a constant disconnection from our true Self (physical, spiritual and emotional needs). Emotional immaturity has contributed to the rise in social anxiety today. The excessive focus on an appearance on social media and the undue obsession for "views and likes" just to satisfy the raging desire to be seen and heard.

Other concerns of the emotionally immature ones are the fear of being misunderstood, fear of not being accepted, fear of being rejected, etc. This fear captures our sense of identity with the perceived approval or disapproval of others.

For many Self Healers, the awareness of our way of living exposes us more to the cyclical patterns of individuals around us. Healing takes day-to-day commitment and has to be chosen. A major achievement of emotional maturity is knowing how to be peaceful with being misunderstood.

Boundarylessness doesn't allow maturity to thrive. As you keep expanding in life, learn ways to tolerate differences, contrast is a trademark of emotional maturity. There is the *"ninety-second rule"* of emotions. It states that our spiked emotions last for only a minute and a half and then it is over. The human body craves to always return to homeostasis.

To cope with emotional maturity involves soothing. It is best to deal with discomfort as we cope and endure.

A NOTE FOR PARENTS

The way emotional maturity can be nurtured within, the same can happen to children. Parent figures are to do this to build the emotional maturity of all they are head over;
-   Take out time and energy to take care of yourself.
-   Preserve your body and learn ways to harness the power of your nervous system response, gain entrance into your authentic self, exemplify emotional control and flexibility. This way the child learns through coregulation.

- Make sure you remain in a balanced and self-expressed state to help the child manage dysregulation more, deal with their emotions better, and using you as a safeguard when he needs to return to safety.
- Encourage your child to attempt self-care and loving discipline by physical activity, alone time, quality sleep, and more.
- Help your children make sense of stress when it appears but explaining the feelings they feel and why it is a normal sensation to their mannerisms.

INNER EMOTIONAL MATURITY BEAMS OUTWARD

We need to be more self-accountable. The stronger our faith grows in Self; the more temptations we will encounter. So prepare to fail, prepare to fall off the track; but do know that the path we began still exists and all we need do is go back to the drawing board and continue the race for holistic wellbeing. It is up to us to be self-accountable, this way we are empowered to succeed.

- **Lessons**
1. Emotional immaturity is the incapability to tolerate.
2. The feeling of emptiness often streams from a constant disconnection from our true Self.
3. Other concerns of the emotionally immature ones are the fear of being misunderstood, fear of not being accepted, fear of being rejected, etc.

- **Issues surrounding the subject matter**
1. Why doesn't boundarylessness allow maturity to thrive?

_____

_____

_____

_____

_____

_____

_____

_____

- **Goals**
1. How can we be more self-accountable to becoming emotionally mature?

_____

_____

_____

_____

_____

_____

_____

_____

- **Action steps**

1. To develop emotional maturity and resilience, we are to;
- Reconnect and discover our emotions such as; practice body connection meditation, carry out an emotional body check-in...
- Assist our body to return to balance such as; practice soothing acts such as bathing, self-massage, reading, listening to music, snuggling, moving, expressing emotions, writing...
- Practice enduring activities such as; resting, grounding yourself, engaging in breathwork, spend time with nature, meditate or pray, recite affirmations or mantras, distract yourself, reach out to a professional and get support.

- **Checklist**

1. The goal of the human body is to return to homeostatic balance as fast as possible.

CHAPTER 13: INTERDEPENDENCE

Development and progress never end, when we stop advancing, we start dying. Setbacks come to test our progress and growth in life. When we are faced with stress, implore your coping mechanism tools such as;

- Exercise conscious breathing
- Witness and name the physiological reactions within
- Name the feelings you sense.
- Dwell in your consciousness, witnessing void of judgment and allowing the feelings to come and go.
- Don't allow the evil narrative that crosses your mind to swallow you up.
- Be emotionally mature.
- Set up boundaries to meet with your inner child in a bid to reparent yourself

With a shift in our body, soul, and mind, we create joy, meet with our authentic self, creativity, compassion, acceptance, oneness, and collaboration with the world around us.

FINDING THE SELFHEALER COMMUNITY

Our interdependent Self needs to find a growing community. Being part of a community is core to be well-grounded in your new Self. We can find a mutual community who shares similar interests with us, they can be found in the church, school, in our neighborhood, and even in the fulfillment of our hobbies. In realizing your true self, create boundaries as you learn to reparent. End the toxic relationships hindering you from becoming your best self and make choices in line with your growth only.

There is strength in being part of a community. It helps you to consistently evolve, grow and co-regulate on a large scale. Lastly, it positively affects your mission, vision, purpose, and interdependent Self.

Authentic friendship is a mutual phenomenon and is a connection of remaining separate together. This concerns our emotional, spiritual, and physical needs. An authentic relationship is built on security and both parties or all the parties have a major role to keep the pillars of the relationship standing. Each one of us has a collective role to play and we are responsible for our mind if we are to heal holistically.

Be open and receptive to your new reality. Healing yourself spreads to healing your world and it's your sole responsibility.

- **Lessons**
1. Reconnecting with your soul requires that you explore and reconnect with your deepest desires and wants.
2. To cultivate interdependence, know the areas of your strength, make new choices that are in line with your goal.
- **Issues surrounding the subject matter**

1. How can you practice showcasing your authentic Self as it concerns all areas of your life?

_____

_____

_____

_____

_____

_____

_____

_____

- **Goals**
1. How can you deprogram yourself to be interdependent and evolve into your best Self?

_____

_____

_____

_____

_____

_____

_____

_____

2. How can you reconnect with your soul?

_____

_____

_____

_____

_____

_____

_____

_____

_____

_____

- **Action steps**
1. Balance your mind, your body and reconnect with your soul by being intentional about your food, adequate rest, physical exercise, Self witness, be conscious, recognize your ego stories, note how your self-narratives move your emotional reactions and coping mechanisms.
2. Relate with your inner child daily and reparent wisely henceforth.
- **Checklist**
1. Your holistic healing is your possibility.

CONCLUSION

No one can see the future, we can only make choices today that will have a huge impact on our future; be it good, or bad. The good news is we have our Selftrust, intuition, emotions, and information to help us in making the best of choices. Healing is a must and it begins with your daily choices and the tools used in living life the healthy & right way.

Made in the USA
Monee, IL
28 August 2021